THE CAT
OPERATOR'S
MANUAL

CUS™ Cuddle Unit 5
Domestic Cat

Visit us at
www.cuddleunit5.com

NCBI:txid9685

THE CAT OPERATOR'S MANUAL

Getting the Most from Your New Cuddle Unit

By Queen Olivia III

CHRONICLE BOOKS

SAN FRANCISCO

Quick Start Guide

Foreword

Thank you for choosing Cuddle Unit 5™—we value your trust in us.

Your new Cuddle Unit 5™ will allow you to experience the best in refined biotechnology and premium quality engagement that a pet unit has to offer. We recommend that you read these operating instructions thoroughly so that you quickly become acquainted with your Cuddle Unit 5™ and enjoy all its features.

In addition to explaining how the different features work, we provide many useful tips and information concerning your safety, how to care for your Cuddle Unit 5™, and how to maintain Cuddle Unit 5™'s interest in you. You will also find information on how to snuggle your Cuddle Unit 5™ affectionately and in a psychologically and physically safe manner.

We hope you enjoy your Cuddle Unit 5™ and wish you safe and pleasant petting.

Do not tumble dry

Do not iron

Hand-wash only

Do not dry-clean

Do not bleach

Dry flat

WE ACCEPT NO LIABILITY FOR DAMAGE, OR CONSEQUENTIAL DAMAGE, RESULTING FROM USE OR MISUSE OF THIS PRODUCT.

For people enrolled in "pet-sitting" programs, all instructions for owners apply. Please speak with your designated Cuddle Unit 5™ owner for more information.

TRIP HAZARD

Care must be taken, as Cuddle Unit 5™ may present a tripping hazard* in your household. The risk increases when you are carrying items and unable to see the floor, and peaks when you are juggling several brown paper shopping bags without handles.

*Disclaimer: Cuddle Unit 5™ assumes no responsibility for any tripping-related injuries. Cuddle Unit 5™ is unable to call an ambulance.

WARNINGS ⚠️

- Cuddle Unit 5™ is not a toy, and children should be supervised at all times.

- Cuddle Unit 5™ does not contain any user-serviceable parts and should not be disassembled.

- Avoid "roughhousing" with Cuddle Unit 5™. This increases the risk of being scratched or bitten. It really is silly to train your Cuddle Unit 5™ to be even more violent than its unavoidable fuzzy bloodlust.

- Do not immerse Cuddle Unit 5™ in water.

- Despite what you are seeing on social media, adding a Mini Cuddle Unit 5™ to the household will not improve your Cuddle Unit 5™'s life. Cuddle Unit 5™ isn't lonely; you are.

- If you choose to ignore the previous warning, then Cuddle Unit 5™ may simply move out rather than have their peace and position challenged by a usurper. Cuddle Unit 5™ is very pretty and has options.

- Despite what you are seeing on social media, it is beyond the pale to let Cuddle Unit 5™ casually wander on food-preparation surfaces, not least of all because of the risk of burns from the stove.

- Obviously, if you leave a pan with bacon grease in it on the counter overnight, you are likely to wake up and discover little paw prints and the marks of a lapping tongue. The authors of the manual accept that it's, for all intents and purposes, impossible to keep Cuddle Unit 5™ out of anything. In saying that, steps can be taken, including a clap of the hands and a loud, firm "no" if the perimeter of the kitchen counter is breached in your presence.

BIOHAZARDS

The following warnings deal with medical issues, including brain-altering pathogens, pregnancy, and cat poop. They are included for the fullest picture of the guardianship's responsibilities for Cuddle Unit 5™. The authors do not wish to surprise the reader with information that is jarring when contrasted with the cuteness of the fuzzy features of Cuddle Unit 5™.

Therefore, be assured that while the following information is true and correct, the risks are low if the suggested precautions are followed.

- Cuddle Unit 5™ excreta is a known vector of an infectious pathogen—*Toxoplasma gondii*—which causes toxoplasmosis, an infection known to cause rats to lose their fear of Cuddle Unit 5™. While the effects on humans are still being debated, some have wondered: Could this be the cause of the "crazy cat lady" syndrome?

- If you are immunocompromised or pregnant, avoid changing litter. This is actually good advice for anyone; litter is generally disgusting. If no one else can perform the task, wear disposable gloves and wash your hands with soap and water afterward. Whether immunocompromised, pregnant, or none of the above, as you perform this task, Cuddle Unit 5™ will stare at you with disdain.

- There is the potential for cat-scratch fever to be passed on if your skin is broken by known reservoirs of bacteria. In Cuddle Unit 5™, this includes their mouths and under their claws. Don't feel too superior, though, as the average human mouth is home to six million bacteria, and Cuddle Unit 5™ would like you to keep them all to yourself.

- Clean your hands with soap and water after stroking or playing with your Cuddle Unit 5™. If you have been scratched or bitten, immediately wash the area with soap and water. Cuddle Unit 5™ cleans frequently, and so should you.

- Don't mess with Cuddle Unit 5™. Cuddle Unit 5™ may or may not mess with you depending on the vagaries of their psychology.

- Cuddle Unit 5™ is a furry force of nature.

CONTENTS

Startup Chime

Cuddle Unit 5™ can be woken from sleep mode by lightly touching any part of its touch-sensitive body.

The startup chime is played upon power-up, before trying to engage the motive system. This sound indicates that Cuddle Unit 5™ has run internal diagnostics and found no faults, and in a few minutes will be completely alert.

Exterior Overview

(View A)

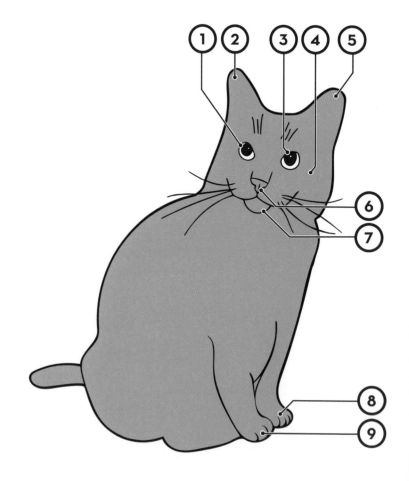

1. Judgment emitter (right)

2. Directional-attention indicator (right)

3. Judgment emitter (left)

4. Scritch zone 1

5. Directional-attention indicator (left)

6. Humidor

7. Furry chin

8. Left slasher, in stowed position

9. Right slasher, in stowed position

Exterior Overview
(View B)

1. Antennae 1

2. Audio out, propellant port (half duplex)

3. Antennae 2

4. Pat zone start

5. Pat zone middle

6. Scritch zone 2

7. Pat zone end, scritch zone 3

8. Temperature port, poop chute (half duplex)

9. Emotional-state indicator

10. Fine-emotional-state indicator

11. Rumble unit

12. Danger zone

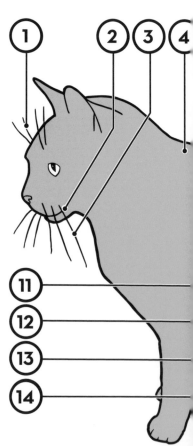

13. Right launch assembly/eviscerator

14. Left launch assembly/eviscerator

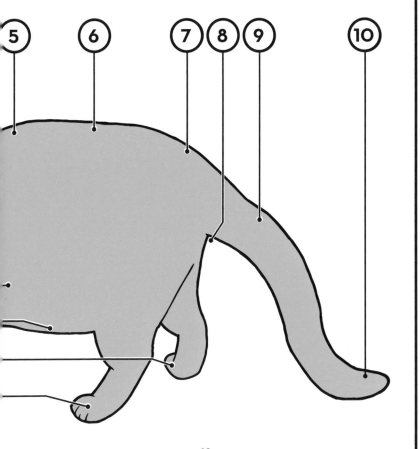

Interior Overview

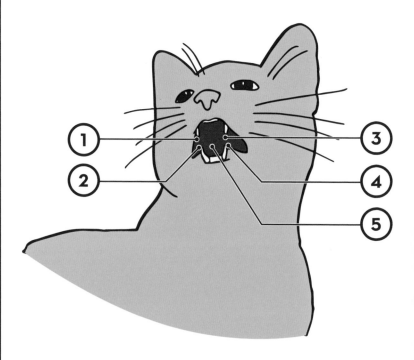

1. Right saber

2. Right impaler

3. Left saber

4. Left impaler

5. Gaping maw of doom

WARNING

Keep hands well clear of Cuddle Unit 5™'s mouth; bites can happen without provocation, and all teeth are capable of piercing human skin.

If you are bitten, immediately flush the area with water to reduce the risk of infection. Deep wounds require immediate medical attention by a specialist.

Central Processing Unit (CPU)

1. **Nap Coordination Center:** Manages all aspects of the napping schedule and preferences, which will always be convenient for Cuddle Unit 5™ and perhaps less so for you. Cuddle Unit 5™ may locate their nap atop the book you are trying to read, or time their nap so that there are no cuddles for you when you arrive home from work, and conversely zoomies commence at 2 a.m.

2. **Laser Pointer Obsession Lobe:** Dedicated to the elimination of the infernal red dot.

3. **Food Demanding Cortex:** Operates on a continuous loop, which runs slightly shorter each day with the goal of moving tomorrow's breakfast back to tonight, with an extra breakfast tomorrow too.

4. **Random Object Batting Nucleus:** Drives the urge to swat pens, spectacles, ornaments, moths, rodents, and, sometimes, your toes.

5. **Affection Decision Node:** Uses a sophisticated non-deterministic scheduler that keeps everyone guessing, alternating between icy aloofness and irresistible displays of affection.

6. **Bloodlust Nexus:** Cuddle Unit 5™ is a hunter, and this is the motive force.

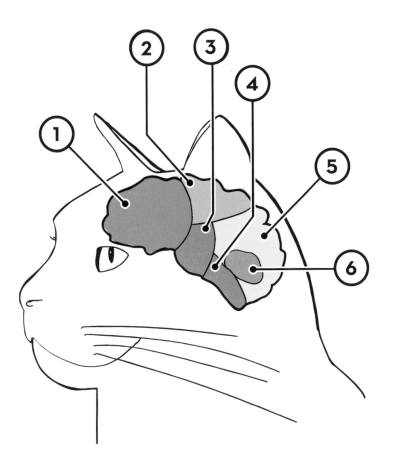

Mood Mode Indicators

Cuddle Unit 5™ is optimized for muscular efficiency, requiring far fewer facial muscles than humans. Body language and vocalizations are the primary signals of mood mode.

Study this documentation closely and familiarize yourself with the efficient non-facial emotional-communication style that comes as standard equipment with all Cuddle Unit 5™ systems. Doing so will enhance your enjoyment of Cuddle Unit 5™.

1. Standby Mode

2. Disappointed Mode

3. Eco Mode

4. Murder-Death Mode

5. Hungry Mode

6. Fur-Ball Vomit Mode

Judgment Emitters

Bright light

Normal lighting

Low light

Ultra-violence

High beam

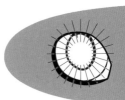

Slow Blink

The communication protocol between multiple Cuddle Unit 5™s is primarily visual, with body language taking the lead. Supplementary audio protocols (hissing and growling) may be deployed. See: Sounds (p. 30).

In the absence of hissing and growling, Cuddle Unit 5™ may wish to bestow upon the viewer the gifts of trust and acceptance. For this, the body language protocol is the slow blink.

Human operators are encouraged to use this gesture to communicate trust and friendship with their Cuddle Unit 5™.

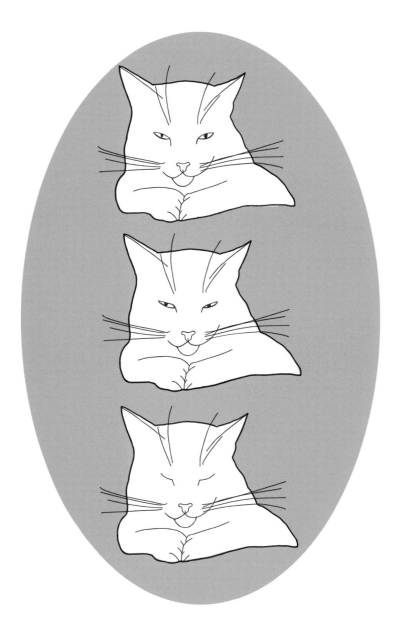

Sounds

Meow

The standard sound emitted by Cuddle Unit 5™ is the ono-matopoeic "meow." It is recommended that interpretation of this utterance be coupled with a read of body language to completely understand the meaning of the communiqué.

Cuddle Unit 5™s with more mature operating systems do not meow to one another in the wild. It is a vocalization usually between parental units and their smaller counterparts, and in this way, your Cuddle Unit 5™ condescends to you with every look they take and every sound they make.

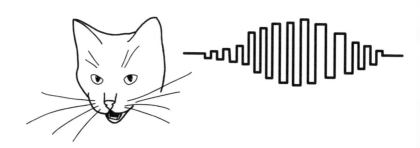

Chirp

Most commonly, this is the chirp that indicates all systems are fully operational and functioning normally.

It may also be a moment of supreme psychological manipulation, as Cuddle Unit 5™ turns up the cute to 110% to obtain treats and pats. Refer to: Startup Chime (p. 14).

Yowling at Unseen Spirits

Also known as "singing the song of my people," this haunting air is often heard at 11:30 p.m., just as you are about to drop off to sleep.

When confronted, Cuddle Unit 5™ will revert to standard meows.

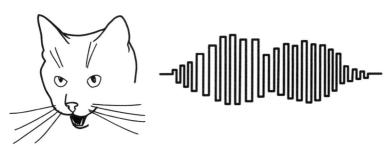

Meoooooooow

This vocalization indicates that Cuddle Unit 5™ is near death from hunger, and why is dinnertime not five minutes ago, you absolute monster.

See also: Protest Poo (p. 72).

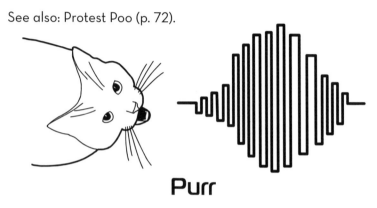

Purr

The gentle rumble of the contented Cuddle Unit 5™ is an absolute delight.

Idling at between 25 and 150 hertz, this vibration has been observed to increase bone density and encourage healing.

Kneading may also be present.

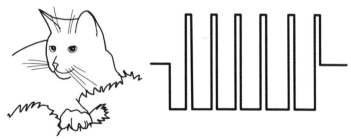

Growl

If Cuddle Unit 5™ is growling, the best course of action is to keep your distance.

Refer to: the Sharp Embrace™ (p. 62).

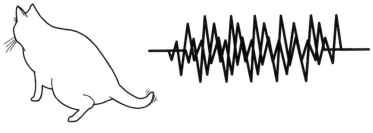

Hiss

Cuddle Unit 5™ is generally tolerant, but there are limits, and once exceeded, a loud and slightly terrifying hiss may be expressed on no uncertain terms.

Hissing Cuddle Unit 5™s should not be approached unless you are rendering first aid.

See also: Medication (p. 120).

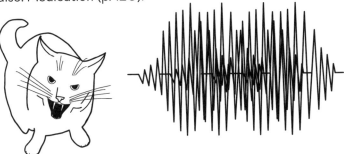

Toe Beans

1. Dew slasher
2. Jelly
3. Carpal whiskers
4. Carpal bean
5. Pinto
6. Launchpad
7. Mung
8. Coffee
9. Soy

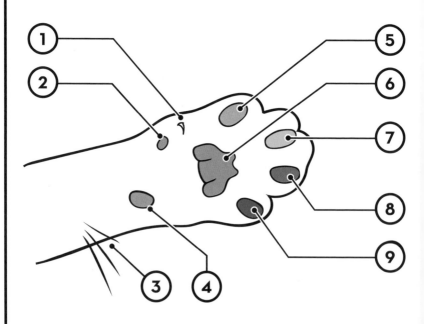

WARNING

Photographing Cuddle Unit 5™'s toe beans requires skill and wit. Approach with caution, as sudden movements, or sounds, may cause a sudden swipe, bite, or a high-speed escape.

First establish that Cuddle Unit 5™ is in a relaxed mood. Then gently approach the paw with your lens, focusing on the precious toe beans, but be ready to retreat at the first twitch of the tail. Toe beans are a highly sensitive area, and this invasion of personal space may be met with sharp resistance. But the reward of a successful toe bean snap is surely worth the risk.

Stretched Feet

Periodically, Cuddle Unit 5™ will enter stretching mode, which keeps the multitude of muscles, tendons, and bones that make up the motive and high-efficiency propulsion system at peak readiness for murder games and zoomies.

As part of this self-maintenance process, the Cuddle Unit 5™'s feet will be stretched, and each of the toe beans will be spread widely, as to take the biomechanical systems to their furthest limit.

A side effect of this process is the emission of a cats-boson field. This field is harmless; however, should you look at it with your eyes, your hands will begin interacting with the field in a predictable fashion, which is described below.

You will feel a compulsion to place the tip of your index finger between the furry gaps that are opening between the toe beans and emitting this invisible, but irresistible, cats-boson field.

If you do make contact with the furry gap between the toe beans, the cats-boson field will collapse, and the feet will return to their stowed position.

There is a risk that Cuddle Unit 5™ will not appreciate the cats-boson field being collapsed by your probing finger. In this case, you may experience an instant boundary and receive a bite on the softest part of your hand.

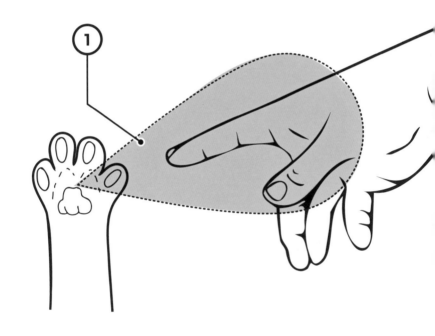

1. Cats-Boson Field

Making Biscuits

During Cuddle Unit 5™'s developmental phase, the kneading behavior (also known as "making biscuits") was an automated response that stimulated the flow of propellant from the parental unit. This behavior also strengthened the bond with the parental unit.

This kneading behavior will be activated when Cuddle Unit 5™ detects comfort and security parameters at optimum levels for snuggles with a human operator (or comfort object, such as a fluffy blanket or your freshly laundered cashmere sweater).

The slasher assemblies will engage in a rhythmic pressing motion, mimicking the propellant flow stimulation technique from the developmental life-imprinting data. The soft toe beans will precisely sense the pressure setting.

It is advisable for human operators to use a protective layer, such as a blanket, to avoid the slasher assemblies from causing a pinprick sensation in your skin. Not only protecting yourself from discomfort, this also ensures that the bonding process remains a positive experience for all involved.

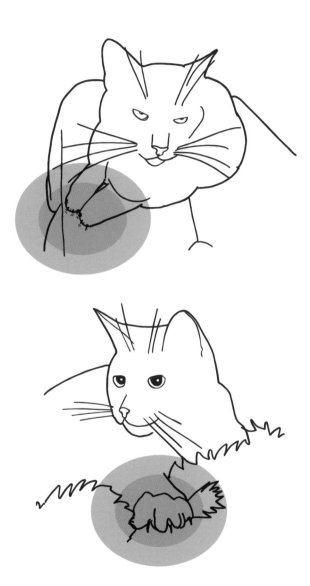

Propellant

Cuddle Unit 5™ is quite content when fed veterinarian-quality kibble. Cuddle Unit 5™ will be happy and healthy and, most importantly, won't be a furry menace at mealtimes.

Cuddle Unit 5™ has a strong fondness* for supermarket wet food. If you don't mind being pestered by an insistent unit during mealtime and running the risk of a Level 2 Protest Poo, by all means indulge them.

When it comes to little pouches of treats, Cuddle Unit 5™ lacks self-control. Cuddle Unit 5™ is quite capable of eating so much, so quickly, that they might make a "vom" right where they're located, say, on the couch, where your friend is sitting.

Cuddle Unit 5™ is lactose intolerant, and a milk meal will likely result in an unfortunate mess, perhaps on your bed. Are you willing to take that chance?

Cuddle Unit 5™ is wild about cheese, like, "I'll do absolutely anything for cheese, but I won't do that" level of enthusiasm. Except, unlike the afore-misquoted lyric, Cuddle Unit 5™ will "do that," repeatedly and creatively. Happily, for Cuddle Unit 5™, the lactose content of cheese is significantly lower than that of milk. When coupled with a far-smaller serving size, Cuddle Unit 5™ is unlikely to befoul your soft furnishings after consumption of just a tidbit.

Cuddle Unit 5™ requires constant access to clean water. They prefer shower water above all, so after you clean the shower, make sure you thoroughly rinse away any cleaning products. Cuddle Unit 5™ must not ingest any toxic toilette chemicals.

Cuddle Unit 5™ will beg for treats when you are cooking. Offer them a morsel, even if it's not something they would typically eat. They'll either enjoy the snack or leave the kitchen, realizing that you consume some peculiar things (e.g., fruit). However, do not offer more than one treat, or you may create a persistent issue, or more accurately, a noisy tripping hazard in the kitchen.

*"Strong fondness," of course, is a euphemism for "addiction," and it is no joking matter. Twelve-step groups for wet-food-addicted Cuddle Unit 5™s do not exist, but they should.

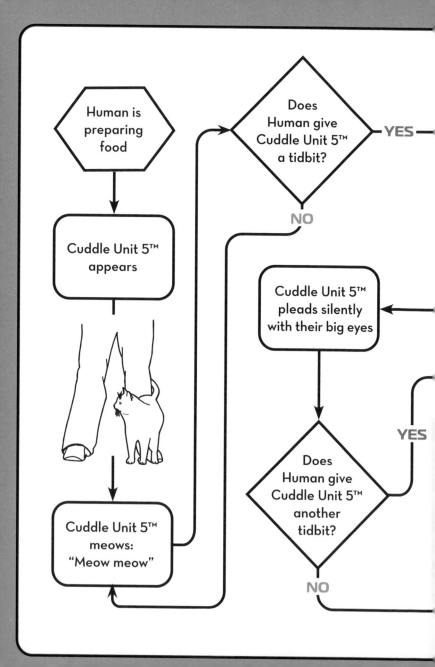

Human is preparing food

Does Human give Cuddle Unit 5™ a tidbit? — YES —

Cuddle Unit 5™ appears

Cuddle Unit 5™ pleads silently with their big eyes

NO

Cuddle Unit 5™ meows: "Meow meow"

YES

Does Human give Cuddle Unit 5™ another tidbit?

NO

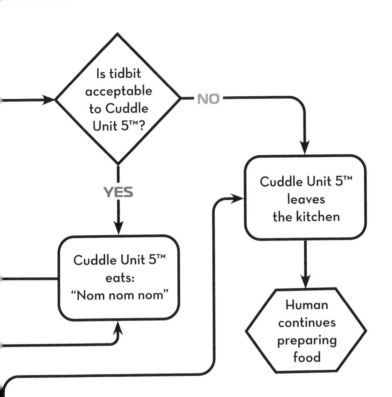

Cuddle Unit 5™ can and will befriend every retired old lady in your neighborhood, then mysteriously put on loads of weight and come home smelling of grandma perfume.

Understanding: This Is an Empty Bowl of Food

Cuddle Unit 5™ is displeased when plain porcelain is visible in their food bowl. At all times, Cuddle Unit 5™ perceives this as a state of emptiness and will behave accordingly. Do not attempt to understand this logic; it is beyond our human comprehension. Simply provide more kibble and be grateful for the blessings of Cuddle Unit 5™.

Cuddle Unit 5™ may manipulate a multi-human household into providing extra food. In this situation, the first person awake should place all the kibble for the day into a container out of reach, then only fill the food bowl from this supplementary food vessel. This approach ensures that everyone is aware of how much food has been provided in a day, and each person can experience the satisfaction of pleasing the unit by offering kibble, hearing the crunching, and enjoying the purring of a contented Cuddle Unit 5™.

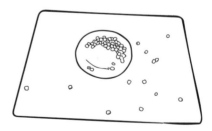

Entomophagy

Although kibble comes in flavors such as beef, chicken, and salmon, Cuddle Unit 5™ would be happy for the alternative flavors: moth, cricket, and unidentified beetle. Cuddle Unit 5™ is a bug connoisseur. Not only are bugs quick-moving playthings, but they are also a nutritious protein-rich snack. So don't be alarmed if your Cuddle Unit 5™ is munching on a crunchy insect; it's all part of life's rich tapestry.

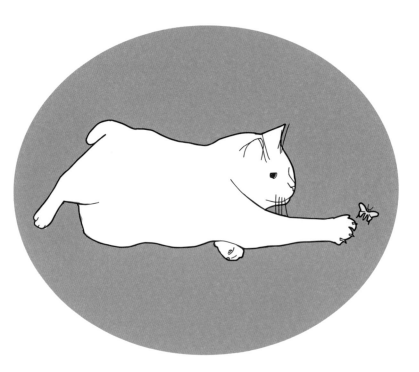

Bidirectional Ownership

The saying "Dogs have owners, cats have attendants" is quite inaccurate. You serve Cuddle Unit 5™ only to the extent you're willing. You assume the role of "the assistant," yet, paradoxically, you remain in control because you are fourteen to twenty-one times larger than a Cuddle Unit 5™ and possess opposable thumbs.

There are many ways to assert your authority—also known as "leading from a supporting position." Here are three suggestions, in order of increasing finality:

1. Refuse food if Cuddle Unit 5™ pleads at the table.

2. Confine Cuddle Unit 5™ in the bathroom for a limited period.

3. Exit the home, go for a walk, have a coffee (or alternative noncaffeinated beverage), visit friends. Get some perspective.

Under no circumstances should you allow yourself to be at the mercy of Cuddle Unit 5™, lest you suffer the fate of a certain roommate. Said roommate was conditioned by Cuddle Unit 5™ to be an on-demand petting machine. After several years of this, the roommate emerged from their bedroom, cradling Cuddle Unit 5™ in a fluffy blanket. With tears in their eyes, they told the owner, "I can't pet your Cuddle Unit 5™ anymore."

Due to this roommate's inability to establish adult boundaries with Cuddle Unit 5™, this human had been pushed beyond their emotional limits in giving pats and affection to Cuddle Unit 5™. Cuddle Unit 5™ was indifferent to their suffering.

You absolutely must maintain the role of the responsible party in the relationship, the one with opposable thumbs; otherwise, Cuddle Unit 5™ will take charge and turn you into their servant. Of course, if that's your preference, remember—the safe word is *kibble*.

Standby Mode

Cuddle Unit 5™ will enter Standby Mode automatically when falling asleep.

Cuddle Unit 5™ has a polyphasic sleep pattern, sleeping multiple times a day rather than all at once, all night long.

Cuddle Unit 5™ naps are around an hour plus fifteen minutes. In total, Cuddle Unit 5™ will sleep between twelve and twenty-two hours a day.

The amount of time spent asleep will increase as Cuddle Unit 5™ ages.

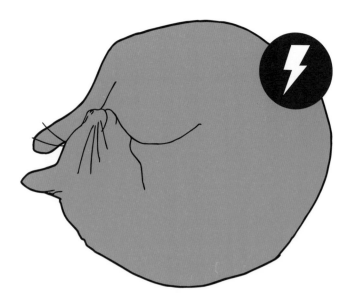

Cuddle Unit 5™'s circadian rhythm is crepuscular, with waking activity peaking at dawn and dusk. This neatly coincides with the activity patterns of their prey animals. But, in a human home, it fits in well with the breakfast and dinner rituals of the (sub)urban *Homo sapiens*. In the wild, Cuddle Unit 5™s are small enough to be prey to larger animals like bears and coyotes. So when they sleep, they minimize their vulnerability by seeking hidden nooks out of sight, such as inside a discarded shipping box from an online retailer. Yes, the box is more appealing than that expensive carpet-covered cat tree.

Conversely, the Cuddle Unit 5™ will sprawl—sunny-side up in a sunbeam—for hours, secure in the knowledge that humans have destroyed its predators' habitat with several thousand square miles of tract housing, freeways, and office blocks.

When Cuddle Unit 5™ Standby Mode is prematurely interrupted, they will emit a startup chime. See: Sounds (p. 30).

Eco Mode

When Cuddle Unit 5™ is awake, they will generally be operating in Eco Mode, in which the speed of their mental processing is slowed to preserve energy.

In this efficient mental state, Cuddle Unit 5™ will stand, seemingly for hours, while you hold open the door. Why is Cuddle Unit 5™ taking so long to decide? Because, in Eco Mode, their brain is running at a reduced refresh rate.

A side effect of Eco Mode can cause a prone Cuddle Unit 5™ to slip and/or fall off your lap after getting their balance wrong.

Eco Mode will also result in Cuddle Unit 5™ looking at you blankly when you are calling their name, frantic, because you are now both running late for a vet appointment.

Decision time is increased in Eco Mode.

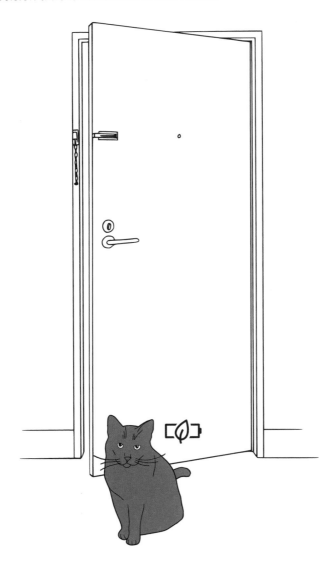

Turbo Mode

Cuddle Unit 5™ will enter Turbo Mode when required. This mode uses so much mental and physical energy that Cuddle Unit 5™ will spend most of their life asleep, and when they are awake, in a state of near-mental stupor, so that when Turbo Mode is activated, the unit has the stored reserves that give them godlike reflexes and speed.

Triggers for Turbo Mode include the following:

1. Prey animals such as birds, mice, or bugs

2. String that is moving like a prey animal

3. The sound of kibble rattling

4. Electric can openers

5. The smell of cheese

6. Sudden and/or loud noises

7. Snakes and cucumbers behind them

8. Laser pointers

9. The sound of you returning home

10. Wiggling your toes under the bed sheets

Turbo Mode Activation

Eco Mode

Sound activation

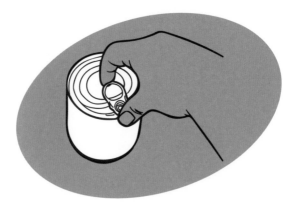

Turbo Mode activated

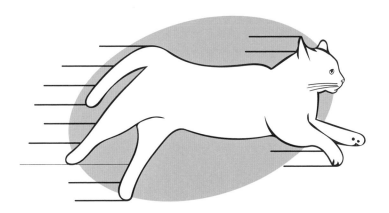

Propellant ingestion

Zoomies

Cuddle Unit 5™ is equipped with battery-conditioning technology to prevent a runaway-thermal event. Zoomies are not to be confused with Turbo Mode. Read on to discover the differences between these two high-energy events.

Cuddle Unit 5™ is equipped with a sophisticated subsystem to manage energy levels. In the event of their internal battery being overcharged, the zoomies sequence will be initiated. Once initiated, Cuddle Unit 5™ will bounce around the lounge like an absolute loon, with eyes like dinner plates as excess power is burned off in the primary-motive systems.

This increase in internal wattage may also cause disruptions to the sensory-processing centers, which may result in Cuddle Unit 5™ standing stock-still, poised for madness, staring at unseen adversaries. Much like a large language model, Cuddle Unit 5™ will give the appearance of suffering from hallucinations.

No additional steps need to be taken while the zoomies process proceeds to its natural conclusion.

Solar Charging

The Cuddle Unit 5™ is a hybrid-electric unit. As such, they can maintain the homeostasis of their core body temperature by supplementing the heat generated by endothermic-biochemical reactions with infrared energy from the sun. In short: solar charging.

Depending on the length of time Cuddle Unit 5™ charges for, it is possible that patting the angel hair of the soft tummy-tum-tum will activate the Sharp Embrace™. Therefore, care is required when approaching Cuddle Unit 5™ while they are conducting a solar charge.

This is a particular danger when the operating temperature is raised, as solar radiation floods Cuddle Unit 5™'s exterior housing.

Secure Sleep Mode Compartment

Your Cuddle Unit 5™ prefers to enter Sleep Mode in well-fortified locations, and cupboards (sometimes drawers)—especially those containing soft (preferably freshly laundered) clothes, towels, or bedding—are favorite places.

Cuddle Unit 5™ may also teleport into a cupboard (see: Teleport, p. 64). If your Cuddle Unit 5™ is missing at mealtime, it is worth checking the linen cupboard, the closet, and any drawers that are frequently opened. Cuddle Unit 5™ can spend hours tucked away, but it's possibly best to ensure these spaces have their doors left ajar so that Cuddle Unit 5™ can readily access water and the litter tray.

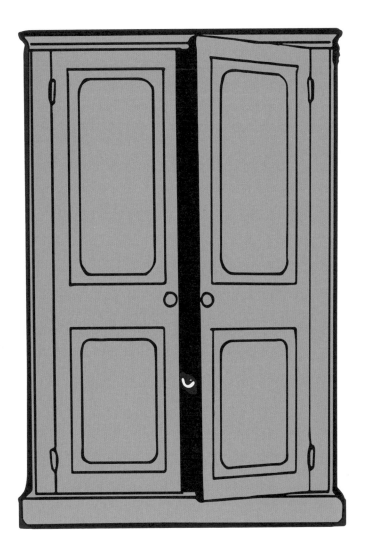

The Sharp Embrace™

As the bear trap ensnares the unsuspecting, so, too, can the Sharp Embrace™ of Cuddle Unit 5™ capture your hand if it becomes the target of aggression while petting the warm, soft, angel hair of their belly.

If this occurs, the best course of action is to avoid struggling, as doing so will only provoke Cuddle Unit 5™ to claw more intensely, kick more furiously, and bite down with greater certainty. Their ultimate goal is to eviscerate your hand as if it were the soft underbelly of a small rodent morsel. Cuddle Unit 5™ longs to disembowel and feast on the innards of its unfortunate prey. In this case: your hand.

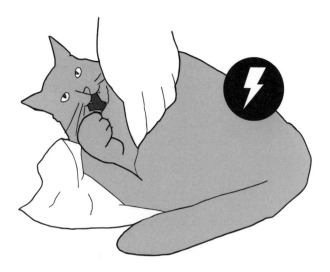

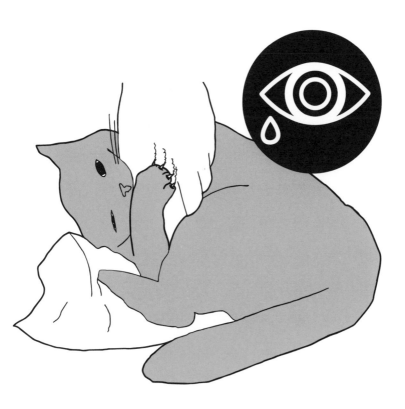

Following the Sharp Embrace™, it is advisable to wash your hands and apply antiseptic ointment, then cover with bandages. For any deep puncture wounds, seek medical advice without delay.

Teleport (beta)

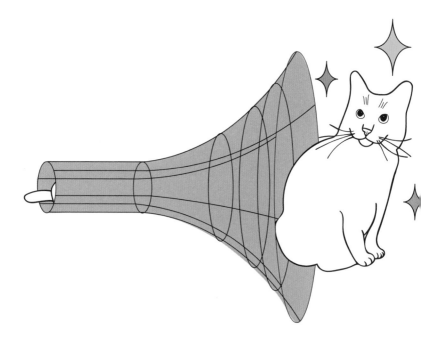

Cuddle Unit 5™ comes equipped with the beta version of the site-to-site teleportation subsystem. This allows Cuddle Unit 5™ to perform short-range teleportation by dematerializing, skimming atop the quantum foam in a non-corporeal energy form, and then silently rematerializing right behind you. See: Trip Hazard (p. 8). This will most likely be synchronized with your time at the kitchen counter.

As this feature is still in beta, though, there will be times where teleportation may be an obvious advantage (ex. being shut in cupboards), but it may fail to engage. Much as you must keep your hands on the steering wheel, you must always remain alert to the needs of Cuddle Unit 5™.

Due to the quantum-observer effect, it is impossible to perceive the de-materialization/re-materialization in progress, but you can be assured that the system is fully operational if, and when, you find yourself thinking, "How the heck did Cuddle Unit 5™ get there?" as you trip backward while holding a bowl full of batter.

It is worth noting that if Cuddle Unit 5™ appears to be stuck in some high-up place, such as a tree or the roof, and is yowling for your help, it's possible that they have teleported there. Your observation of their corporeal form may be preventing teleport from engaging. In this situation, the best thing to do is to leave the scene, which will enable the de-materialization sequence to initiate so that Cuddle Unit 5™ will remove themselves from the high-up place.

Note: If Cuddle Unit 5™ remains stuck for more than thirty minutes, then you should seek a ladder, or the fire department, to come to assist.

Window Surveillance Protocol

At set times of each day, Cuddle Unit 5™ will take up sentry in the front window, maintaining a vigilant watch of the front yard (or similar, depending on the nature of your home).

This will include the vital task of avian activity observation, with associated real-time commentary in the form of chattering, a vocal inflection that sounds like a repeated, rapid, high-pitched staccato. If we were to transcribe it, we might write "eh, eh, eh, eh!" This will frequently be accompanied by intense focus and twitching whiskers.

This activity is excellent for providing mental stimulation and provides hours of self-directed entertainment. It may also sate some of the bloodlust that lurks in the soul of your Cuddle Unit 5™, providing a harmless outlet for the killer instinct (even if the chattering sounds too cute to come from a killing machine).

Closed Door Protocol

You will soon come to understand that a closed door is intolerable to Cuddle Unit 5™. This goes double for the bathroom door. Like the moment in a horror film when the monster locates the hero, you will be innocently making your morning ablutions when one paw, then two, come clawing under the door.

It is unclear why Cuddle Unit 5™ is so drawn to you at your most vulnerable and intimate moment of repose atop the porcelain throne; however, it is a fact that Cuddle Unit 5™ longs to be beside you at this time and receive much praise and attention.

Despite Cuddle Unit 5™'s excellent sense of smell, there is not an odor produced by your digestive system that will deter Cuddle Unit 5™ from enthusiastically joining you when you are attending to the call of nature.

Comfort Optimization Algorithm

Once Cuddle Unit 5™ has identified a soft, quiet, and still place to achieve their daily quota of twenty-two hours of sleep, they will activate the Comfort Optimization Algorithm (COA).

Do not disturb Cuddle Unit 5™ while this algorithm is running, as doing so will reset the algorithm and restart the COA from the beginning.

COA enables Cuddle Unit 5™ to identify and position their body to achieve maximum comfort. Cuddle Unit 5™ will circle the identified sleeping area several times, with each rotation allowing their paws to assess the softness and stability of the sleeping surface.

Once COA is complete and Cuddle Unit 5™ has achieved maximum slumber comfort, it is imperative that you do not move (under penalty of the Sharp Embrace™) until Cuddle Unit 5™ decides they have had enough rest and hops off of their own accord.

The Aft Section Cuddle

This Cuddle Unit 5™ cuddle configuration is one of deep affection. Your thigh has been chosen for contact by the fluffy butt of Cuddle Unit 5™ as they slumber. Rejoice in the warmth and acceptance, and under no circumstances should you attempt to move (or cough too loudly).

You can try a pat (pictured), but there is a non-zero chance that this additional contact will lead to the hasty conclusion of aft-section cuddle time.

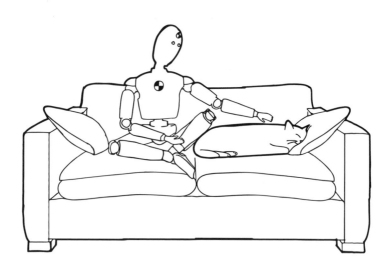

The Landing Gear Cuddle

This rare gesture indicates Cuddle Unit 5™ approves of your existence (for the moment). This acceptance is born of your utility as a maintenance strut during scheduled exterior cleaning.

Do not try to extend the duration of the landing gear cuddle, as adorable as it may be, as this could very well result in triggering The Cold Shoulder Maneuver (p. 84). Remain still and enjoy the softness of the landing gear and the knowledge that you are being touched by the toe beans.

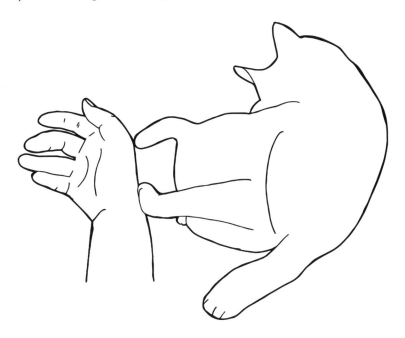

Protest Poo

There will be times in your relationship with your Cuddle Unit 5™ when you must assert boundaries that may displease them. However, in these moments, Cuddle Unit 5™ may lack the physical strength or the advantage of opposable thumbs to resist your directives. In such instances, the Cuddle Unit 5™ might decide that revenge is a dish best served cold. Cold, and squishy.

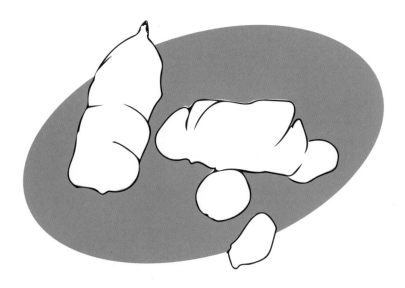

Enter: the Protest Poo.

There are two categories of Protest Poo. The first—and the most common—is the secret Protest Poo. In this case, Cuddle Unit 5™ will discreetly deposit their waste under your bed, in a corner, or at the back of your closet. It's only the odor—or worse, the sensation of cold cat poo squishing between your toes—that alerts you to its presence. This is an exceptionally effective form of communicating extreme displeasure.

The second, less common Protest Poo is the Live Poo Event™. This begins when Cuddle Unit 5™ enters your field of vision while remaining out of reach. Maintaining direct eye contact, Cuddle Unit 5™ will squat and contract their abdomen to release the foul product of their bowels. When you have committed an exceptionally egregious offense, Cuddle Unit 5™ may also yowl simultaneously. There can be no doubt about the simmering furry fury being communicated in this moment.

The following actions on the part of the human have been known to elicit a Protest Poo:

1. Removing the litter tray and insisting that it's time for Cuddle Unit 5™ to do their business outside because they're six years old and a grown-up now

2. Going on holiday

3. Returning home from a holiday

4. Moving a favorite blanket or other soft item that Cuddle Unit 5™ has previously made a sleepy nest on or in

5. Bad weather

6. Serving the wrong cat food

7. Loud noises

8. Children

9. Moving furniture around in the room

10. Allowing a strange dog on the property

11. Allowing a strange human in your bed

A Note on the Litter Box

It should be noted that failing to maintain a clean litter box (if your unit lives indoors) may result in poo and urine everywhere except the litter box. In this case, it isn't a Protest Poo, but rather a Cry-For-Help Poo. If you ever experience this, you should burn with shame,* as it is your responsibility to provide a clean environment for Cuddle Unit 5™ to do their business. If this happens repeatedly, it's likely that you are incapable of properly caring for Cuddle Unit 5™, and you should consider re-homing them to a place where they will receive the love and clean environment they need to thrive.

*The authors do not care what your therapist says; in this scenario, you *do* deserve to feel terrible.

Protest Poo Zones

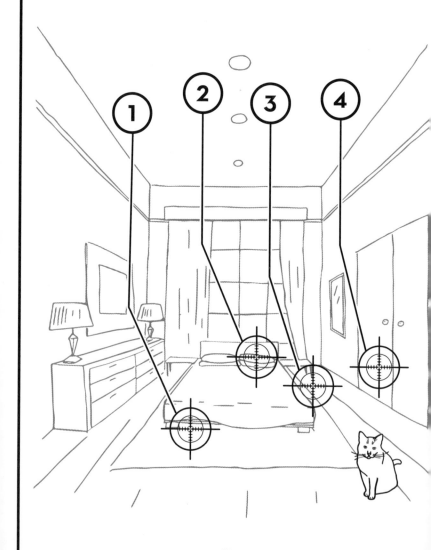

1. Under the Bed

It will be furry before it is found, after much sniffing and asking household members: Do you smell something funny in here?

2. The Pillow

Communicating maximum displeasure.

3. Next to the Bed

This will be deposited in the dead of night to be trod in upon awakening, the cold poo squishing between your toes, and you will know you were wrong to change the brand of your unit's propellant.

4. Back of the Closet

Typically, this will be discovered when you are dressing for a wedding, smeared on the hem of your most formal garment, too late to dry-clean; the message will resound loud and clear.

Precious Carpet Gifts

1. Bathroom (tile)

2. Bedroom 1 (carpet)

3. Bedroom 2 (carpet)

4. Half bath (tile)

5. Kitchen (tile)

6. Lounge/dining (hardwood)

7. Rug (shagpile)

a. Cuddle Unit 5™

b. Precious carpet gift (your foot pictured)

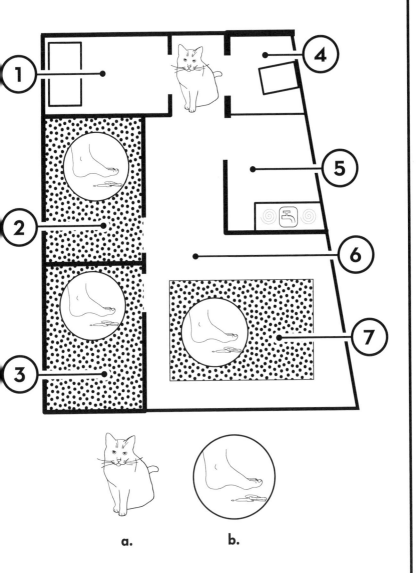

a.

b.

Precious Carpet Gifts

Cuddle Unit 5™ possesses a biofuel-digestion subsystem tuned to digest high-fat and high-protein propellant. Like a high-performance sports car, Cuddle Unit 5™ is exquisitely sensitive to the composition of the ingested propellant.

Fortunately, should Cuddle Unit 5™ consume propellant that isn't of the correct composition, a fuel-dumping procedure is initiated. This may be hurried along by the consumption of ordinary grass, which is known to catalyze this procedure.

In the wild, Cuddle Unit 5™ goes to great trouble to conceal its existence from predator and prey animals alike. This includes keeping a well-groomed coat, so as not to advertise a smell. Further to this is their penchant for burying their waste. Well then, how to discreetly dispose of dumped fuel (also known as "cat vom") in a hurry? The answer, of course: a good chunder in the long grass.

Now that Cuddle Unit 5™ occupies a (sub)urban home, the floor covering that most resembles the historically discreet receptacle of half-digested kibble is the carpet, rug, flokati, or, if you are very unlucky, the eiderdown comforter.

Therefore, Cuddle Unit 5™ will make a quick beeline to your soft furnishings before completing the retching evaluation of repellant propellant.

Cleaning up is quite simple. Scrape up the solids with a dessert spoon. We recommend this spoon be dedicated to this unholy duty and is stored away from the kitchen cutlery. Then flood the area with water and place a folded towel upon the watery mess. Stamping on the towel with your body weight will cause the water to be absorbed into the towel. Alternate between flooding and sopping up the diluted liquid with dry towels until no trace of evacuated propellant remains. In a few days' time, when all the liquid has evaporated, the area can be treated with a dry carpet shampoo.

The authors of this book can testify to the efficacy of this strategy, having never once lost a security deposit on a series of rentals, all in which this process had been repeated many, many times.

Human Avoidance System

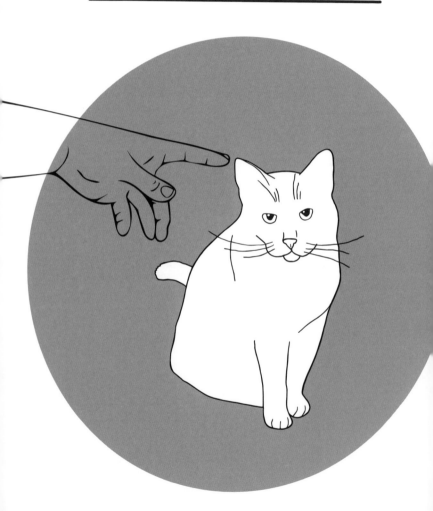

Once Cuddle Unit 5™ is equipped with LIDAR, that ensures they can stay a Planck length* away from your probing hand when you desire to pet Cuddle Unit 5™ at a time that is not on their furry agenda for that exact moment.

L – Look,

I – I know you want to fondle me.

D – Don't do it. I'm

A – Asking nicely but if you persist,

R – Really sharp pain will be yours.

"Go ahead, make my day."

* The Planck length lᴘ is defined as:

lᴘ = Planck length

ℏ = Reduced Planck constant

G = Gravitational constant

c = Speed of light in a vacuum

$$l_P = \sqrt{\frac{\hbar G}{c^3}}$$

*The Planck length is the smallest measurement that can be accurately made at the quantum scale. Shorter lengths exist, but their measurement becomes uncertain due to the nature of the quantum realm, and Cuddle Unit 5™ will not tolerate the ambiguity.

The Cold Shoulder Maneuver

Through no fault of your own, your Cuddle Unit 5™ will frequently assume the cold shoulder posture, which is to have their back to you and ignore every utterance, entreaty, high-pitched trilling, and poorly articulated meow, as well as any amount of *psss psss psss psss*.

This is not a malfunction; sometimes Cuddle Unit 5™ prefers a reality where you do not exist. It isn't personal (mostly).

This is just a very special way of communicating "While I may acknowledge your presence, I can just as easily choose to ignore it." Don't take it to heart.

Ending the Cold Shoulder Maneuver is as simple as rustling the treats bag, which will immediately return you to the center of Cuddle Unit 5™'s universe.

Self-Cleaning Mode

Self-Cleaning Mode is activated when three or more humans are gathered in a room together, such as for a potluck dinner, or virtually, such as for an important video call with your boss, senior staff members, and an HR representative. When Cuddle Unit 5™ detects this critical mass of humanity has been achieved, the algorithm will begin and follow the following phases:

1. Cuddle Unit 5™ will enter the room and come near all the humans assembled but not close enough for a pat.

2. Once this perimeter has been established, Cuddle Unit 5™ will calculate the point that is equidistant from all those assembled, then saunter to that location.

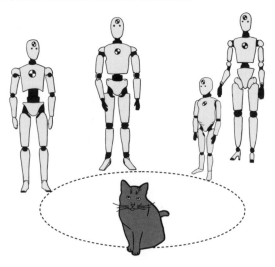

3. Cuddle Unit 5™ will simultaneously, and slowly (this program runs in Eco Mode), raise one hind leg to the eleven-o'clock position while the other hind leg stretches out to the nine-o'clock position, and the tail to the three-o'clock position.

4. Cuddle Unit 5™ will then lower their head to the point where the two clock hands would meet and proceed to lick, and chew, the fur around their temperature port to ensure its complete hygiene.

5. This will continue for some time, typically until at least half of the assembled humans are looking away in embarrassment. Embarrassment is a social emotion that is not a feature of Cuddle Unit 5™.

6. Once the temperature port is completely cleaned, Cuddle Unit 5™ will do one more lap of the assembled humans to reestablish the perimeter of the "you can't quite reach to pat me" zone, then leave.

Edges

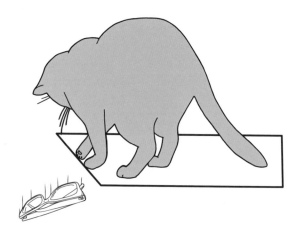

Cuddle Unit 5™ maintains, at all times, a precise internal register of which of your personal items are most precious to you. It is likely that spectacles, keys, and smartphones are jockeying for top place in this list, but it could include a special china cup, makeup, or dental appliance.

In the case where insistent vocal warnings have been ignored—and this is especially true leading up to the mealtime—Cuddle Unit 5™ may engage in Knocking Precious Things off the Edge to rouse you into action.

Direct eye contact is optional, but the general approach is for Cuddle Unit 5™ to gently extend a front paw and softly, and so innocently, bat at the precious object that is near the edge. Using an internal "back off" algorithm, Cuddle Unit 5™

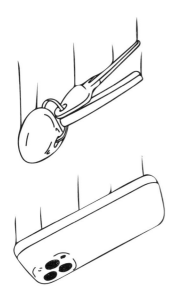

will pause for various lengths of time to give you the opportunity to meet their fuzzy needs, and if you fail to do so, soft, gentle batting will commence.

The upshot of this is that your Precious Thing will advance, almost imperceptibly, toward the Edge, culminating in your Precious Thing being knocked off and falling to the floor.

Do you have tiles? Does your smartphone have a rugged case? Are your spectacles now shattered? Irrespective, Cuddle Unit 5™ will meet your exasperated gaze with cool indifference and may even begin scouting for the next item to gently pat toward the abyss.

The quickest way to end this is to get up and make sure that kibble covers the entirety of the food bowl.

Murder Games

Cuddle Unit 5™ is a hunter, and play is a game of mutilation and death.

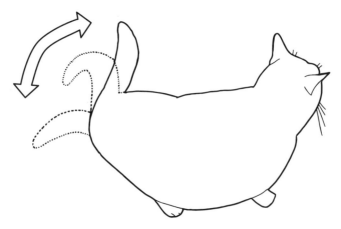

Cuddle Unit 5™ is a sprinter, not a marathon runner. Stalking prey is part of the fun, building furry tension. Then some unquantifiable state of arousal passes an internal threshold, and the small, sharp, violent anger is expressed.

In this diagram, a roll of paper towels is eviscerated and left for dead. Like an afternoon thunderstorm in the desert, it is over as soon as it begins, and only the faint twitching of the tail and the wry angle of an ear are left as evidence of the papery-tissue carnage.

Cuddle Unit 5™ in the Workplace

Cuddle Unit 5™ will join any work (or personal) video call that you care to initiate. This is not optional. Other parties on the call would like to see Cuddle Unit 5™ (and those who don't shouldn't spoil the fun for those who do). So make sure you hold up Cuddle Unit 5™ to the camera and take the meeting off-topic for at least ten minutes.

Note: Video-conferencing technology interferes with the Human Avoidance System, resulting in Cuddle Unit 5™ being "all over you like a rash" when you are trying to be professional on a work call.

Collaborative Bed-Making

Cuddle Unit 5™ is a highly motivated bed-making assistant and will appear as soon as you begin to apply clean sheets to any bed. Once this activity commences, bed-making becomes a team sport, as Cuddle Unit 5™ variously capers, pounces, and buries themselves within and beneath the clean linens.

It may be that the teleport subsystem has been engaged, as the moment you have removed Cuddle Unit 5™ from the mattress protector so that you can spread out the fitted sheet, Cuddle Unit 5™ has broken at least a few rules of physics and is now, somehow, under the mattress protector, having gained access despite the tight tuck.

Be prepared for endless rounds of repositioning and adjusting as your furry assistant ensures that bed-making is never a solitary endeavor.

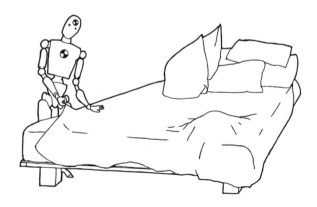

The Clean Laundry Protocol

The clean laundry protocol will be initiated when Cuddle Unit 5™ detects the folding and sorting of freshly laundered garments. Upon entering the laundry zone, Cuddle Unit 5™ will deploy to the summit of the laundry pile, or as we say in the lab, "scaling Mount Clean Washington."

The clean laundry protocol will be scheduled as high priority, and attempts to distract or dissuade Cuddle Unit 5™ from scaling the heights of your hand-washed delicates are unlikely to succeed.

Toys

Cuddle Unit 5™ is interested in things that resemble prey:

1. Ping-Pong balls

2. String that twitches across the horizontal plane of their field of vision

3. Plush mice and fish

4. A roll of paper towels or toilet paper

5. Any part of you that, under the bed covers, appears as a small rodent trying to avoid annihilation

6. Your big toe

All these things can excite Cuddle Unit 5™ into Turbo Mode, and then the carnage begins as the red mist of the furry berserker descends.

To prolong playtime with Cuddle Unit 5™, consult the pounce-to-kill-ratio graph below and ensure you keep within the optimal range for amusement and Ping-Pong-ball devastation.

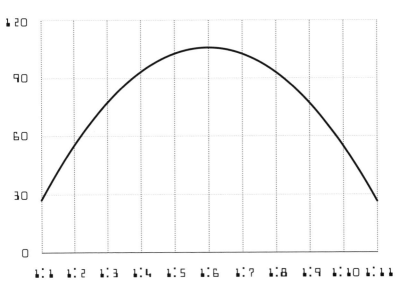

Pounce: Kill ratio
- Playtime (seconds)

Lasers

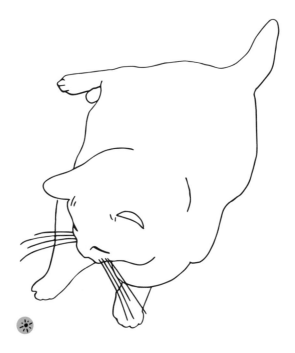

For the couchbound, a laser pointer provides a fun way to activate Cuddle Unit 5™'s furry rage, to unleash the violent bloodlust that is so very entertaining in the (sub)urban lounge. Obviously, it is important to use a low-power laser because lasers pose a very real risk to the eyesight of any mammal. Perhaps it's safest to purchase the laser from a pet store.

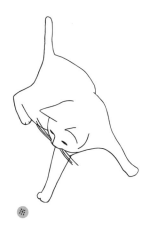

Tracking

Once activated, the laser play will last as long as Cuddle Unit 5™'s frustration threshold is not exceeded. Because, you see, the hunt for the infernal red dot becomes a mockery of the annihilation potential of play, as there is quite literally nothing for Cuddle Unit 5™ to sink their sharp little teeth into. No soft underbelly to tear asunder with rabbit-kicking hind legs.

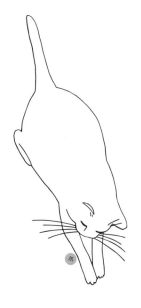

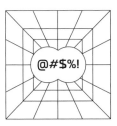

@#$%!

If you are committed to playing laser from the couch, then it is over when Cuddle Unit 5™ decides it is over. Though, if you can rouse yourself, finishing the game off with a favorite physical toy, be it "stringy string" or the "plush birdie on a plastic rod," and letting Cuddle Unit 5™ descend into the depths of murderous evisceration, it's likely you will be able to keep the interest in the laser pointer that much longer.

Robotic Vacuum Cleaners

Will Cuddle Unit 5™ voluntarily clamber aboard your robotic vacuum cleaner and ride around your living room like a space-age shagpile sailor?

The compatibility between Cuddle Unit 5™ and various robotic vacuum cleaners can vary. Due to this variance, the interaction between Cuddle Unit 5™ and the vacuum will fall into three major categories:

1. Fluffy futuristic Valkyrie atop a robotic vacuum cleaner

2. Disinterest

3. Avoidance

Cuddle Unit 5™ offers no guarantees or representations about performance while in proximity to any brand of robotic vacuum cleaner. As they say in the auto industry: Your mileage may vary.

Boxes

Cuddle Unit 5™ loves sitting in a box. In the wild, Cuddle Unit 5™ could be a snack for a coyote, a bear, or a hawk, and so an instinct to find a protected spot to sleep is strong. Enter the cardboard box—the snuggest, most secure enclave. Cuddle Unit 5™ will transgress several laws of both classical and quantum physics in order to install themselves in even the smallest box. As the old adage goes, "If I fits, I sits," for values of "fits" all the way down to the Planck length. See: Planck length (p. 83).

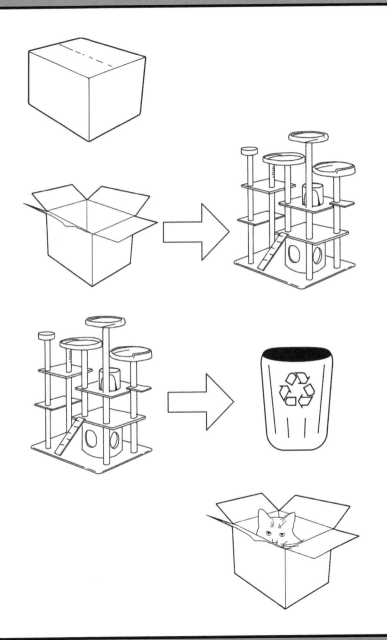

High-Value Scratching Posts

It is imperative to provide Cuddle Unit 5™ with a scratching post, or scratching pad, for without access to claw conditioning surfaces, Cuddle Unit 5™ will surely turn to higher value items, such as the vintage leather sofa of your roommate's late Nana.

Despite your best efforts, Cuddle Unit 5™ may eschew your proffered scratching items, instead turning their slashers to the task of efficiently eviscerating your soft furnishings, drapes, and other beloved fabric-covered items. If this is the case, the only solution is to remove the items entirely, or to fashion some kind of protective covering.

It is said that aluminum foil will deter Cuddle Unit 5™ from scratching; however, most interior design experts agree that aluminum foil is not a fetching accent for any decor scheme, and as a material it is best reserved for covering casseroles.

Mine

Cuddle Unit 5™ reserves the right to sit on any chair, at any time, and shed any amount of fur. Any human who subsequently sits in such a chair will have this fur transferred to their own garments. The only way to avoid this is to put blankets or towels down on all the chairs, but now you live in a house with blankets and towels on all the chairs, and you forget to lift them up most of the time, and even when you do, somehow the fur still got on the chair.

It's easier just to accept it.

Fur Decontamination

Within no time at all, your entire habitat will be home to thousands of fine shedded furs, from your sofa to your bed and certainly all your knitwear.

To remove the fur, there are two recommended strategies: One is the venerable sticky roller, which can be run across the surface of fur-contaminated garments with increasing desperation to try to uplift the pernicious fur. The other is to live with it and accept that the only function of your washing machine is to more evenly distribute the fur across your entire wardrobe.

Mobile Heating Pad (Interior)

To a human, it may be thousands of dollars' worth of laptop, perhaps even belonging to a human employer. It is an essential tool for anyone navigating the modern workforce. But to Cuddle Unit 5™, this is simply a mobile heating pad.

To avoid testing if your work laptop is rated for eleven pounds of cat, it is recommended that laptops are either put away in their carry case when not in use or leaned against something on an angle, like a guitar in repose.

Mobile Heating Pad (Exterior)

To the human, the automobile is an essential mode of transport, but to Cuddle Unit 5™, when the automobile arrives back on the property, warm from its internal combustion, it is a glorious exterior mobile heating pad. Irrespective of street parking or an internal garage, Cuddle Unit 5™ will optimize their internal temperature with the addition of the waste heat of the cooling engine radiating through the hood.

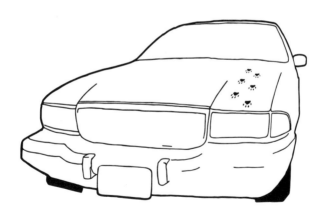

Recreational 'Nip

There is a variety of flowering plants in the *Nepeta* genus, 'nip
(Nepeta cataria) and 'mint *(Nepeta racemosa)* being the most
fascinating to Cuddle Unit 5™. They are also known by their
street names: "the nip," "snip," and "meowie wowwie."

These pretty little plants with purplish white flowers contain
within them a substance called nepetalactone. This substance
is a terpene (like turpentine), and is released when the plant is
damaged, crushed, or chewed upon. Its function to the plant
is to act as an insect repellant, but it also has an effect on
Cuddle Unit 5™.

66.6% of all Cuddle Unit 5™s are equipped with olfactory receptors that are sensitive to the compound nepetalactone. Once triggered by the inhalation of the substance after crushing the greenery, β-endorphins are secreted into the bloodstream of Cuddle Unit 5™. These endorphins then bind to μ-opioid receptors.

You don't need a bachelor's degree in chemistry to spot the words *endorphin* and *opioid* to get an idea about how great your Cuddle Unit 5™ will be feeling after its brush with catnip. Like, super great—like, really, really, really great.

They will rub and rub upon the leaves, releasing even more of the terpene as they ascend ever further into the highest planes of euphoria.

Once under the influence of "meowie wowwie," Cuddle Unit 5™ will purr, and rub, and look around maniacally for invisible ghosts. They will careen around the room, neglect their responsibilities, miss bill payments—in short, their furry lives become unmanageable. However, effects are only temporary.

Eventually, a short-term tolerance is built up, and they can't get any more wasted despite their best efforts, and after the high-speed zoomies, they will sleep it off.

This substance isn't addictive, especially compared to wet food or cheese. But it is exceedingly pleasurable, so if you've planted it in your garden, prepare for its untimely demise.

As mentioned earlier, there is no refining process needed to ensure the potency of 'nip. It doesn't have to be dried, or cooked, or baked into brownies because the bonding of the active compound to the Cuddle Unit 5™'s pleasure center starts in the nose via the terpene vapors of "the nip."

Stages of intoxication:

- Crazy eyes
- I can't get enough of this stuff
- OMG purring this is amazing!
- Zoom zoom zoom
- Crash and sleep (Standby Mode)

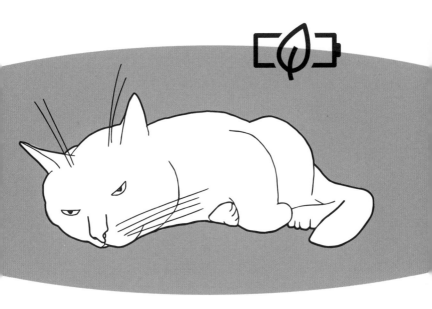

The Covenant

The human–Cuddle Unit 5™ relationship is enshrined by the extrajudicial dictum of the Covenant. Established in the First Dynasty of ancient Egypt, circa 3100 BCE, it was founded on the excellence of ancient Egyptian cats' ability to catch and dispatch the vermin attracted to granaries, which served as storage places for surplus grains.

This soon led to cats deigning to allow humans to pet and fuss over them, and before long, the concept of the Cuddle Unit 5™ relations with humanity bloomed forth like the blue lotus on the Nile.

If and when your Cuddle Unit 5™ presents the fruits of their hunt—the lifeless body of a small rodent, the tail of a skink (a type of small lizard), or the still-twitching carcass of a sparrow—you must remember: This is the Covenant, the reason that the unlikely relationship between a small, solitary carnivore and a noisy, social ape has lasted over six millennia.

What you do with the corpses is up to you. Throwing them down the gully is perfectly acceptable, as is wrapping them in a paper towel and tossing them into the neighbor's garbage.

Veterinary Concerns

Ensure that you form a relationship with your local veterinary practice, take Cuddle Unit 5™ in for annual checkups, and follow all advice given.

With the correct care and maintenance, your Cuddle Unit 5™ will provide you with years of enjoyment and entertainment, and remember: You will get out of this arrangement what you put into it.

Slasher Maintenance

To maintain peak slashing performance, Cuddle Unit 5™ will activate slasher maintenance several times a day. The targeting systems will identify a surface of rough texture and firm resistance, and the Cuddle Unit 5™ will repeatedly plunge in and yank out the slashers. This action serves to keep the tips needle-sharp.

If you don't want the arms of your upholstered chairs looking like they have been in a knife fight, it is advisable to purchase either a scratching pole or a scratching pad. Both items can be sourced in any good pet-supply outlet.

It is not recommended to declaw Cuddle Unit 5™, as after-market modifications will void your warranty.

If Cuddle Unit 5™ leads a mainly indoor existence, then regular trimming of the slashers is advised. This should be done carefully, as claws contain a blood supply. In the first instance, have your veterinary nurse demonstrate at the same time you purchase a claw-trimming tool.

If Cuddle Unit 5™ is spending time outdoors, then the normal wear and tear of tree bark and rugged terrain should be sufficient to keep the slashers at their optimal length.

1. Cuticle

2. Quick

3. Slasher

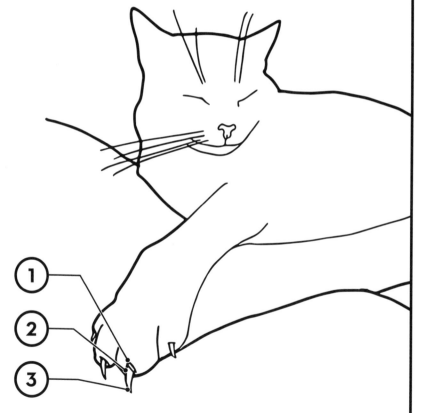

Medication

Sometimes you are going to have to administer pill-based medication to Cuddle Unit 5™—worming tablets, antibiotics, and maybe other pharmaceuticals as prescribed by your vet.

1. Left hand

2. Aux. left hand

3. Pill

4. Gaping maw of doom

5. Aux. right hand

6. Right hand

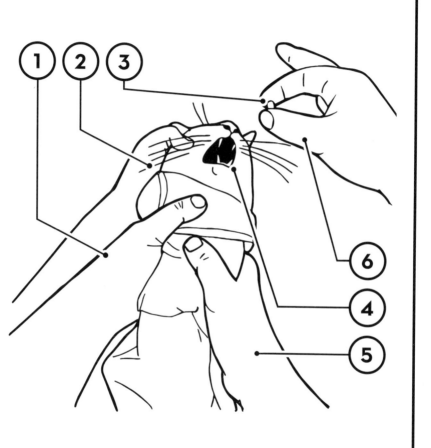

121

Medication

Cuddle Unit 5™ is about as enthusiastic to orally receive a pill as a teenager is to put their phone down at dinnertime.

The best strategy is to wrap Cuddle Unit 5™ tightly in a blanket, creating a burrito and thus rendering all eighteen of the slashers inoperative. Then there is only the sharp dentition in the gaping maw of doom to contend with.

The process is quite simple. Approaching Cuddle Unit 5™ from behind, using your left and right hands, hold a towel taut and quickly wrap it, left over right, around Cuddle Unit 5™'s body. Do this tightly, like you see at your local Mexican restaurant when they assemble a burrito. Burrito de gato style.

Now that Cuddle Unit 5™ is snuggly wrapped and immobilized, preventing a violent outburst, it's likely that Cuddle Unit 5™ will begin emitting devil noises—low, evil growling that sounds like the soundtrack to Revelations.

Keep the burrito de gato snug with your left and right hands, lest the furry fury be set loose and eviscerate your person.

Now, using your auxiliary left hand, reach from behind Cuddle Unit 5™'s head and gently press into the cheeks with your thumb and index finger, causing the gaping maw of doom to be moved into the open position.

Now, using your auxiliary right hand, gently deposit the pill into the farthest reaches of the gaping maw of doom and simultaneously release your auxiliary left hand to begin stroking

Cuddle Unit 5™'s throat to stimulate the swallowing reflex.

Release all four of your hands, collapsing the burrito de gato, and you are done. Congratulations.

Note: If Cuddle Unit 5™ takes two steps and spits out the pill, you'll need to redo this process from the start.

System Diagnostics

Problem	Cause
Cuddle Unit 5™ runs into the bathroom meowing. If you follow them in, they may sit on the bath mat and continue to meow.	Cuddle Unit 5™ is a bit itchy, and they have decided it's time for brushy-brushy.
Cuddle Unit 5™ lures you into the bathroom with meowing and then stands in front of the shower door.	Cuddle Unit 5™ thirsts.
You are in bed, and Cuddle Unit 5™ is walking around and around and around, and a-meowing.	Cuddle Unit 5™ wants snuggles.
Cuddle Unit 5™ is meowing at you a lot.	The food bowl has naked porcelain glaze exposed.

Remedy

There is a cat brush in the cupboard under the sink. Give Cuddle Unit 5™ a good brush, and don't forget to give their cheeks a scritch.

Open the shower door and run the cold water for a while. Leaving the door open, shut off the water, then let Cuddle Unit 5™ enter to lap away at eau de toilette.

Lie in the human recovery position, and Cuddle Unit 5™ will make a nest for themselves on the arm you have outstretched.

Replenish food bowl with kibble. There is no limit to the amount they eat, so consult the packaging, or your vet, for the appropriate portions.

**Dedicated to Sophie Cat, the original #CuddleUnit5,
who crossed the rainbow bridge May 26, 2022.**

To my pocket internet friends who selflessly reviewed the draft
before I sought representation: Virginia, Fiona, Kris, Mari, Jane, Kate,
Cathie, Sara, Tim, Debbie, Jeremy, Kaz, podsrover.

To the veterinarians who reviewed the draft before we went
to publishers: Dr. Nick Pallin and Dr. Oliver Reeve.

To all the veterinarians, nurses, and staff at Wellington Central Vet Hospital.

To Claire Cavanagh, my tireless agent, who took a chance
on me and my cat comedy.

To Olivia Roberts, my editor who shaped this work into the laughfest
you are holding in your hands now.

To Maggie Edelman, for taking my text and illustrations and creating
a book design that is utterly perfect and completely delightful.

To Kris Roberts and Steve Prenzlauer, who have supported
me throughout my West Coast odyssey, making it an enjoyable
and highly memorable experience.

To Aaron Hilton and Joanne Andrews, for keeping me on an even keel
in New Zealand with regular laughs, phone calls, and sushi.

To Oliver Lineham, Merrin Macleod, and Maru Cat, the best
bubble buddies ever, who helped me out of a real jam during the lockdown.

To Edward Guthmann and Lucy Dog, who gave me
excellent advice on writing.

To Meliors Simms, where would I be without our weekly
writers check-ins? Probably not published! Thank you for keeping me
honest and for all the fantastic suggestions.

To my parents, Jessie and Alastair Johnston, who had three sons and two
cat children named Candy and Abby. Who taught my brothers and me the
wonder, the love, and the comedy in the bond between us and the cats.

Library of Congress Cataloging-in-Publication Data

Names: Queen Olivia, III, author. | Johnston, Conrad, author.
Title: The cat operator's manual : getting the most from your new
cuddle unit / by Queen Olivia, III.
Description: San Francisco, California : Chronicle Books LLC, [2025] |
Represented by Conrad Johnston.
Identifiers: LCCN 2024029707 | ISBN 9781797232324
Subjects: LCSH: Cat owners–Guidebooks. | Cats–Behavior.
Classification: LCC SF447 .Q44 2025 | DDC 636.8–dc23/eng/20240711
LC record available at https://lccn.loc.gov/2024029707

Manufactured in China.

Design by Maggie Edelman.

10 9 8 7 6 5 4 3 2 1

Chronicle books and gifts are available at special quantity discounts to corpo-
rations, professional associations, literacy programs, and other organizations.
For details and discount information, please contact our premiums department at
corporatesales@chroniclebooks.com or at 1-800-759-0190.

Chronicle Books LLC
680 Second Street
San Francisco, California 94107
www.chroniclebooks.com